Behavior Games

and beyond...

play games...change behavior!

By Tracy Milanese, MS

The author can be contacted at tlmilanese@outlook.com

Book Design by Tracy Milanese and
Longfeather Book Design
LongfeatherBookDesign.com

ISBN 978-0692676905

DEDICATION

This book is dedicated to my children who not only helped me test out these games, but also helped create the actual book.

Charlotte, age 10 • Illustrator
Calvin, age 13 • Editor
Kassie age, 15 • Photographer

Table of Contents

And Beyond...

Introduction

This book contains a new approach to helping kids learn appropriate behavior. Traditional games have been assigned to common behavioral issues in children. It is designed for young children (ages 3-9) and a wonderful way to work with special needs children of all ages. Choose a behavior that needs to be developed or modified and play the corresponding game. Using games to develop desired behavior meets children on their level which creates acceptance rather than resistance.

It is also much easier to redirect children then to stop them in their tracks. Words like "no" and "stop" can cause children to oppose the direction, but the verbal prompts that are learned from these games redirect without them even realizing it!

Playing selected games helps practice good behavior! The more they play the games, the more reinforced the desired behavior is. Good behavior takes practice and training. What better way to practice good behavior than by playing games?

Behavior Games

Follow Directions

Preparation:

Become familiar with how to play "Simon Says."

What to do:

Teach the child how to play "Simon Says." Once he is familiar with the traditional way to play the game (imitating gestures only when Simon Says), increase the amount of verbal directions. For example: Simon Says "pick up the pillow." Encourage him with verbal praise as he does what "Simon Says."

Goal of the game:

By playing this game, the child practices following directions the first time given. When using Simon Says in everyday situations, such as "Simon Says brush your teeth," it becomes natural for the child to do what "Simon" is saying. Eventually, you can substitute your title: "Mom says pick up your toys." Be sure the child is capable of what is being asked. If the child becomes frustrated or discouraged often while playing, it will turn into a negative experience and not be affective. An example of this might be to say "Simon says stop crying" if he is truly upset.

Used by:

Individuals	Groups/Classrooms	Both
☐	☐	☑

2

Simon Says

Clean Room

Preparation:

Become familiar with how to play "Follow the Leader."

What to do:

Teach the child how to play "Follow the Leader." Once he is used to the traditional way, include picking up his room. You will be the leader and head towards his room (marching is always fun!). As you enter pick up a shirt and put it in a drawer (being sure he is doing the same). Next, pick up his toy and put it in the toy box (he is behind you doing it too). There are no (or minimal) verbal directions.

Goal of the game:

By playing this game, the child practices picking up his room by imitating your behavior. Start with a few things and give verbal praise for copying you when the game is finished. Try to go in the same order each time. For example, put clothes in drawers, toys in the toy box, pillows on the bed, etc each time. This helps him stay organized so eventually he will do it on his own. Part of kids not wanting to clean their rooms is that it is overwhelming. Playing follow the leader each day will keep it under control and create a good routine for him.

Used by:

Individuals	Groups/Classrooms	Both
☑	☐	☐

Follow the Leader

End An Activity

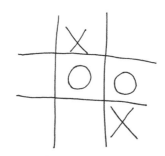

Preparation:

Become familiar with the game "Tic, Tac, Toe"

What to do:

Teach the child how to play this game "Tic, Tac, Toe." For a child who has trouble ending an activity, inviting them to play a short game like tic, tac, toe can be much easier for them. Instead of hearing "stop" they hear "come" which is a much easier transition word.

Goal of the game:

By playing this game the child practices going from one activity to another with more ease. When children are absorbed in what they are doing, they don't want to leave. Especially for some things unpleasant like getting ready for bed! When they have to switch to another short game, it's not as painful. Going from tic, tac, toe to getting ready for bed is easier, because they aren't as engaged in it. It's like a stepping stone! Practicing transitions in steps will make them easier!

Used by:

Individuals   Groups/Classrooms   Both

☐   ☐   ☑

Walk Indoors

Preparation:

Become familiar with how to play "red light, green light."

What to do:

Teach the child how to play "red light, green light." During the traditional game, you need to stop when "red light" is called and run when "green light" is called out. After the child knows the rules of this game if he is running indoors, you call out "red light." He should immediately stop and wait. You would then say "walk."

Goal of the game:

By playing this game the child practices stopping quickly when red light is called if he forgets to walk in the house/classroom. When he goes outside and when it is acceptable to run, yell "green light" time!" Be sure to give a fair amount of "green light" time (which is the most fun for kids!) Give verbal praise when he listens immediately to either command. This works well if a child runs off ahead of you in a crowded store or similar situations when you need the child/children to stop and listen carefully!

Used by:

Individuals	Groups/Classrooms	Both
☐	☐	☑

Red Light, Green Light

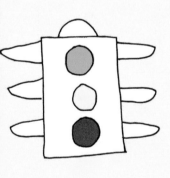

Get Along with Siblings/Peers

Preparation:

Get a Frisbee! (a ball will work too)

What to do:

Teach the child how to play frisbee by demonstrating how to throw it. (If too young, a ball work too). When playing, count the number of times you can go back and forth without dropping it. Next time you play, try to beat the number of catches. Have siblings do the same with each other. Congratulate them when they have worked together to beat their score.

Goal of the game:

By playing this game, the siblings practice working together instead of against each other. It may seem easier to separate siblings who don't get along, however, the more they practice working as a team to reach a goal the better! Give them increasingly difficult activities to work together with such as making cookies for dessert.

Used by:

Individuals   Groups/Classrooms   Both

☐   ☐   ☑

Frisbee

Ball

Honesty

Preparation:

Become familiar with the game "Hangman."

What to do:

Teach the child how to play "Hangman." Play with ONLY statements you sure are true. For example, the hidden words might be "p-u-r-p-l-e-p-e-n-c-i-l" if you are using a purple pencil. Or short sentences for older kids like "I go to school."

Goal of the game:

By playing this game, the child practices saying truthful statements. He also sees his opponent modeling truthful statements. Kids who may have difficulty telling the truth, become more comfortable the more they actually do it. When it comes time for the child to be honest about something he did, the game will allow an easier way to do so. "I-b-r-o-k-e-t-h-e-v-a-s-e." Praise the honesty.

Used by:

Individuals   Groups/Classrooms   Both

✔

Hangman

Eat What's on the Plate

Preparation:

Become familiar with the game "I Spy."

What to do:

Teach the child how to play "I Spy." Play this when he is eating by spying something on his plate. For example, "I spy something green." Child: "Peas?" you say "Yes!" He then has to take a bite of what is guessed. Continue until he is through. He "wins" the game if you can say "I spy an empty plate! You win!" (But really you did)

Goal of the game:

By playing this game, the child practices a fun way to eat what's on his plate. The game takes the attention off of something he may not like. Be sure not to put too much of something he doesn't really like so he is more likely to "win." This keeps the game fun.

Used by:

Individuals   Groups/Classrooms   Both

☑   ☐   ☐

I Spy

Hands to Self

Preparation:

Become familiar with how to play "Hot Potato."

What to do:

Teach the child how to play "Hot Potato." (A pretend potato can be easily made by stuffing a knee-hi with cotton balls and tying the end). As he is playing, be sure to emphasize saying "hot potato" when it comes to you and act like you really don't want to touch it. He will learn to move his hands quickly when "hot potato" is said.

Goal of the game:

By playing this game, the child practices moving his hands away quickly when you say hot potato. When not playing the game, you see him touching his sister's things or hitting his brother, you say "hot potato!" You can also place the hand made potato around the house on things he's not supposed to touch, so it's a visible reminder (your car keys, TV remote, etc).

Used by:

Individuals   Groups/Classrooms   Both

☐   ☐   ☑

Hot Potato

Decision Making

Preparation:

Get some dice!

What to do:

Teach the child odd and even numbers on the dice. Routinely roll the dice to make small decisions: "an odd number means I drink a glass of milk, an even number means I drink a glass of orange juice." Encourage the child to do the same: an odd number means I wear a blue shirt, an even number means the green one.

Goal of the game:

By playing this game, the child practices quick decision making. Some children can get "stuck" when making small, daily decisions. This is a simple strategy that can get their brain "unstuck" and moving ahead. This is just for small, routine decisions not meant to replace the decision making process involved in more important choices.

Used by:

Individuals	Groups/Classrooms	Both
☐	☐	☑

Dice

Tantrums/Aggression

Preparation:

Become familiar with how to play "The Freeze Game."

What to do:

Teach the child how to play "The Freeze Game" by playing music while moving around, then shutting the music off and yelling "freeze." Immediately he stops and holds his position until the music starts, then he can move around again. Start with a few seconds and increase the number of seconds he must keep his body still.

freeze!

Goal of the game:

By playing this game, the child practices controlling his body when you say "freeze." At a later time, if the child is having a tantrum (yelling, stomping feet, etc) you yell "freeze." He stops and after several seconds you say "OK" (in place of putting music back on). Repeat this until the child calms down. Increase the amount of time the child stays frozen. When you say "OK" he can tantrum. The game continues until he is calm, which is how he "wins" the game. This can also work with mild aggression (where no one is at risk for getting hurt).

Used by:

Individuals   Groups/Classrooms   Both

☐   ☐   ☑

The Freeze Game

Quiet Voice/Good Listening

Preparation:

Become familiar with the game "Telephone."

What to do:

Teach the children how to play "Telephone." Think of a simple phrase or sentence and whisper it into a child's ear. He then whispers it to the person sitting next to him and so on. When the phrase is whispered to everyone, the last person says it out loud and if it matches the original phrase, the group "wins."

Goal of the game:

By playing this game, children practice using a quiet voice in a classroom setting. The children have to work together to win the game by waiting quietly for their turn. When the group gets too loud a quick game of telephone will get them refocused. Eventually, a verbal prompt of "use your telephone voice" can be used. The phrase/sentence that is whispered can be a review of what is being taught in class.

Used by:

Individuals	Groups/Classrooms	Both
☐	☑	☐

Telephone

Sharing

Preparation:

Become familiar with the game "Huckle, Buckle beanstalk."

What to do:

Teach the children how to play "Huckle, Buckle Beanstalk." Hide a selected toy, game or treat. The children work together to find whatever is hidden (make it a challenge!) and when they find it they both get to play with it. Remind them that since they both worked to find it, they can both take part in it.

Goal of the game:

By playing this game, the children practice sharing an activity (searching) and an item (whatever they find). Start with something easy to share that doesn't belong to either one of them like a pack of crackers. Eventually, hide someone's own toy and next time the other child's own toy. Practicing working together unites them before sharing.

Used by:

Individuals   Groups/Classrooms   Both

☐   ☐   ☑

Huckle, Buckle Beanstalk

Impulsivity

Preparation:

Become familiar with the game "Bingo."

What to do:

Teach the child how to play "Bingo." Emphasize the need to remain quiet until it's time to call out "Bingo." Explain that you can only win the game when you call "Bingo" out at the right time. Kids who are impulsive want to call out every answer. The chips give them a way to respond to their number using more self control.

Goal of the game:

By playing this game, the child practices waiting before talking out loud. It helps to be able to put the chip down for some of the answers (B-2) and delay calling out until they have several: "Bingo!" Practice this method with other lessons where you would normally ask oral questions and have them raise a hand to answer. Instead, try having them put chips on their answer (create lesson sheets ahead of time) and after they get 5 in a row they can call it out.

Used by:

Individuals   Groups/Classrooms   Both

☐   ☑   ☐

Bingo

Homework

Preparation:

Become familiar with how to play "Dominoes."

What to do:

Teach the child how to play "Dominoes." There are various forms of dominoes: matching the number of dots, matching pictures and matching words. Anyone will do. When is it homework time, instead of transitioning to homework start with a game of dominoes.

Goal of the game:

By playing this game, the child practices matching. This is another stepping stone game. It's easier to go from playing outside to coming inside and playing dominoes, than to come in and go straight to homework. The brain gets "warmed up" by the matching and is easier to transition to higher thinking skills.

Used by:

Individuals   Groups/Classrooms   Both

☑   ☐   ☐

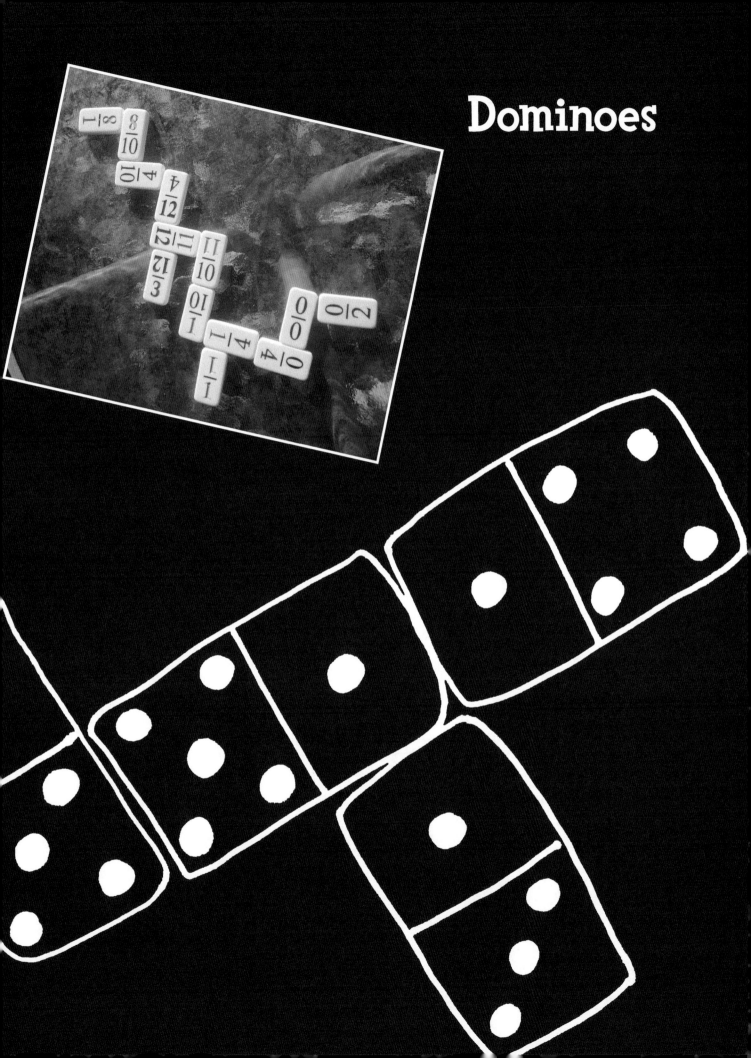

Dominoes

Respect/Manners

Preparation:

Become familiar with the game "Mother, May I?"

What to do:

Teach the child how to play "Mother, May I?" Give a direction (take 2 steps forward) and he must reply "mother, may I?" before he does it. He waits for you to say "yes, you may" and then does whatever was asked. During this game, there is a penalty (going back to the beginning) when permission to do something is not politely asked.

Goal of the game:

By playing this game, the child practices talking respectfully. He learns that the only way to move forward is to ask respectfully. Transition this type of asking to everyday requests. "Mother, May I have some juice." (The wording may be changed to fit your household comfortably. "Dad, may I go outside?" or "Grandma, may I have a cookie.") If it is a reasonable request, the child should be allowed to have what is asked for to reinforce talking politely. If he doesn't ask respectfully, he should be denied and have an opportunity to try again later.

Used by:

Individuals	Groups/Classrooms	Both
☐	☐	☑

30

Schedule/Routine

Preparation:

Become familiar with the game "hopscotch."

What to do:

Teach the child how to play "hopscotch." Write or draw a picture in the boxes underneath the numbers. Put them in the order they are supposed to be completed. This can be used with different types of routines: daily routine, after school routine, bed time routine, etc.

Goal of the game:

By playing this game, the child practices doing things in order. By playing hopscotch with his routine, he has physical and visual reminders of what to do, rather than just verbal cues. This should increase his ability to complete his routine independently.

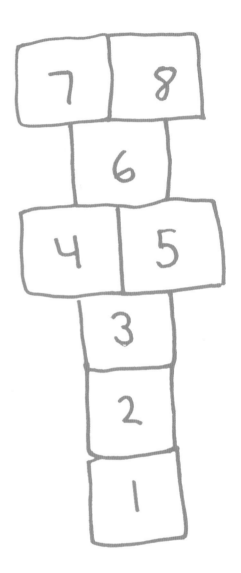

Used by:

Individuals	Groups/Classrooms	Both
✓	☐	☐

Hopscotch

Compliance

Preparation:

Get some puzzles that are appropriate for your child's level.

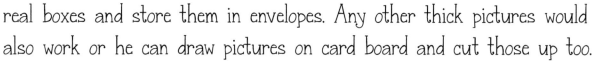

What to do:

Do some puzzles with your child. Store bought ones work great, but if you'd like a variety, cut up some cereal boxes and store them in envelopes. Any other thick pictures would also work or he can draw pictures on card board and cut those up too.

Goal of the game:

By playing with puzzles, the child learns to "comply." For example, if a child misbehaves and is sent to his room, he should be compliant before he returns to his regular activities. Asking him to complete a small puzzle gives an indication of whether or not his mind is ready. If he is ready, he will complete the puzzle and return to whatever he was doing with ease. If there is resistance, he may need more "cool down" time.

Used by:

Individuals   Groups/Classrooms   Both

☑   ☐   ☐

34

Classroom Jobs/Chores at Home

Preparation:

Become familiar with how to play "tag."

What to do:

Teach the child how to play "tag." Ahead of time, write down classroom jobs (or household chores for families with several siblings) on separate index cards. There should be one job for each child playing tag. Each day alternate who is "it." The person who is it, chases and tags the others. When someone gets tagged, he is given an index card that tells his job or chore for that day.

Goal of the game:

By playing this game, the children practice delegating jobs in a fun way. Alternating who is "it" keeps it fair. This is also a great way to clean up after parties, play dates, or sleepovers!

Used by:

Individuals   Groups/Classrooms   Both

☐   ☑   ☐

And Beyond...

A look at how games can connect to deeper issues.

(Not meant to replace treatment of any kind, but may be used in addition to professional help).

Anxious/Fearful

Preparation:
Become familiar with what is causing the anxiety/fear.

Play these games:
Jump rope, solitaire, stacking blocks, matching/ sorting games.

What they practice:
Jumping rope (or any physical exercise) decrease the feelings associated with anxiety. Solitaire, stacking, matching and sorting are all calming activities. They help regulate and organize the body. Practicing physical activities and calming activities will reduce the symptoms of anxiety in children.

Used by:

Individuals   Groups/Classrooms   Both

☑   ☐   ☐

Shy/Withdrawn

Preparation:

Become familiar with what is causing the child to be shy or withdrawn.

Play these games:

Charades, musical chairs, leap frog.

What they practice:

These interactive, group games can offer shy children a way to join the group. Many withdrawn kids just don't quite know how to act in a group setting. Structured games can offer a way for them to practice participating with others. Over time, group games can create the confidence they need to feel comfortable in many different types of group settings.

Used by:

Individuals   Groups/Classrooms   Both

☑   ☐   ☐

Sad/Depressed

Preparation:

Become familiar with what is causing the sadness or depression.

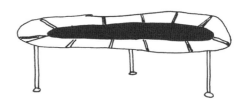

Play these games:

Jump on a trampoline, silly games, (silly songs on a CD or on a DVD) and games that the child is good at. (Avoid competitive, challenging games until depression improves).

What they practice:

Jumping on a trampoline (or any physical exercise) decrease the feelings associated with sadness and depression. Games or songs that promote smiling and laughter will also help decrease these feelings. Playing games the child is already good at will help reinforce the feelings of accomplishment and success, improving self esteem.

Used by:

Individuals   Groups/Classrooms   Both

☐   ☑   ☐

Angry/Irritable

Preparation:

Become familiar with what is causing the child to be angry or irritable.

Play these games:

Tug of war and play dough.

What they practice:

Tug of war is a physical way to release that frustration or anger. Play dough can also be used as a physical release if the child uses it to squeeze, stretch and roll around in his palms. It can also be used as an expressive form. The child can create what is making him angry or use it to get his mind off of the problem for a while if needed.

Used by:

Individuals   Groups/Classrooms   Both

☐   ☐   ☑

ASD/Asperger's

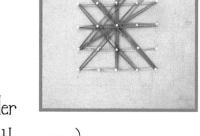

Preparation:

Become familiar with Autism Spectrum Disorder (ASD) or Asperger's. (They are similar, but not the same).

Play these games:

"Feely box" (or other sensory guessing games). Feely boxes can be created by cutting two holes into a cardboard box just big enough for the child's hands to fit into. Put one item at a time into the box and have him guess what it is just by touching it. Increase to more uncomfortable items over time. You can play this type of guessing game with the other senses. Put on a blind fold (or have him cover his eyes) and make different sounds and he can guess what they are. Discuss which ones are pleasant to him and which ones aren't. You can also do this with taste, and talk about the things that tasted good and not so good. A sand or rice tray with small sand toys in it is also recommended.

What they practice:

Feely boxes, or sensory guessing games help the child practice becoming desensitized to uncomfortable or unpleasant sensory experiences. Using a game format (winning the game if he guesses a certain number correctly) makes the experience more fun for him.

Used by:

Individuals   Groups/Classrooms   Both

☐   ☐   ☑

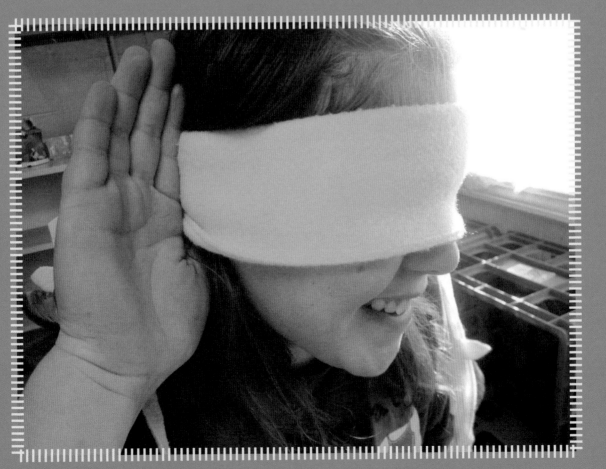

ADHD

Preparation:

Become familiar with Attention Deficit Hyperactive Disorder (ADHD).

Play these games:

Board games, memory, and kite flying.

What they practice:

Board games help the child's impulsivity by practicing waiting between turns. Memory helps the child practice focus and concentration. Kite flying helps the child practice focusing for longer periods of time. It also helps the child's impulsivity because it is hard to quickly stop once the kite is up in the air and it keeps him moving in a forward direction.

Used by:

Individuals   Groups/Classrooms   Both

☐   ☐   ☑

Made in the USA
Charleston, SC
08 April 2016